Dirty talk

Dirty Talk Examples Guaranteed To Drive Your Lover Wild and   Give You Ultimate Pleasure & Excitement for your best moments

EMMA HALE

Contents

Chapter 1

Dirty Talk Expressions

In case you're in a shiny new relationship and figuring out how to turn on your new beau, or you're in a setup relationship, or you're searching for an approach to start up a past love interest, or you're wanting to get into something new soon... well, we're there with you!

Know this early: you're wonderful, you're hot, and there is an explanation people are pulled in to you! We're only here to help with the additional stuff, the icing on the cake. Cake is brilliant, isn't that so? It's tasty; it's filling. Be that as it may, the vast majority need icing on their cake. That is the place where dirty talk comes in. All things considered, icing and dirty talk seem like a magnificent blend; however, we'll get to that later.

You've hit a block with regards to developing the ideal dirty expression to turn on your mate. All things considered, you've gone to the ideal spot. The accompanying guidance, when effectively utilized, won't just turn him on, yet will likewise truly make him insane horny! We should begin.

When to begin?

Timing is of vital significance before you get serious and toss an expression of enthusiasm out there. Keep in mind; wrong planning can generally demolish the disposition! For most people, this could be after a pleasant supper, subsequent to getting into a dirty discussion, and after a couple of glasses of wine. For men - essentially whenever! There is anything but an off-base opportunity to turn on the warmth, except if, obviously, he's in a conference. Also, that being said, dirty content can at present be an extraordinary turn on.

Just hit the correct catches.

At the point when we return home, I will make you arrive at a magnificent climax.

I have to feel you inside me.

I will deplete your balls this evening!

I will stamp you as mine this evening.

I wish I could control myself better around you, yet when I see you, all I need to do is rip your garments off and engage in sexual relations with you.

In any event, when you're feeling awful, you make me horny.

It may sound ravenous; however, I'm horny for your cock so terrible at this moment.

No one has ever screwed me as you do.

On the off chance that we weren't at this gathering and these individuals weren't anywhere near, I would actually bounce on you at the present time!

What might you say on the off chance that I approached you for sex at this moment?

Turn on your mate like there's no tomorrow.

I can scarcely focus; I simply continue considering you snatching me and taking me.

I feel so horny and powerless when you rule me.

I simply need to fold my pussy over your cock.

I will break you today around evening time.

I wore these undies only for you.

Okay, discipline me on the off chance that I was acting bratty?

On the off chance that these individuals weren't here, I would be on my knees with your cock in my mouth.

Realizing that you can actually overwhelm me makes me so insanely horny.

Think about what shading my underwear is?

What might you incline toward I wear today, a strap or underwear or nothing by any means?

Sex and dirty talk about gathering insane speed

Get my bosoms and crush my areolas.

I love it when you screw me like a skank.

I love your dick.

I need to feel your cock in my mouth.

I need to taste your cum.

I need your cum.

I simply need to be your little screw doll.

I would prefer not to be truly ready to walk tomorrow, so screw me harder, mate.

In the event that you do your best, you have some pleasant coming to your direction.

It's a pity we're not in bed right now since everything I can consider is feeling your body on mine.

I've been truly downright terrible should be truly rebuffed.

Making you cum hard is my main need at the present time.

Screw me like you would not joke about this!

Taste me.

This evening we will what I like to do. However, don't stress; it will be loads of fun!

Top me off.

Try not to stop.

Use me.

You will make me cum.

You're not leaving here until I have your cum in my dirty mouth.

Harsh sex when talking dirty

As yet feeling sore after the previous evening.

At times my legs get genuinely powerless when you have intercourse with me.

Cum for me.

I jerked off pondering you the previous evening.

I miss your cock.

Kindly screw me harder, daddy.

Make me your dirty bitch.

Pull my hair and slap me.

Simply considering you makes me so dirty wet!

The sultriest thing about the previous evening was feeling you shoot your heap inside me.

Make a protected sex space when talking dirty.

Choosing a sheltered word or safe expression prior to getting dirty and down to business is a great thought while considering not going excessively far. Realizing limits is the key with the goal that neither one of the parties gets awkward or killed and at last uninvolved. Regarding that picked safe expression keeps up a degree of the shared agreement while wandering into new things, and moreover overlooking the protected expression can change the room into a threatening climate, forestalling the turn on the impact that ought to be related with sex. This is less significant in long haul connections, as it is more plausible you realize how to turn on your mate without intersection any limits. Yet, when you're still in the learning periods of how to turn on your man or lady, there's an equilibrium of avoiding any and all risks and attempting new, insane things you need to learn and dominate. Whenever comfort is accomplished, and you know what's not cool and what's liked - go insane!

Expanding on the establishment of dirty talk

There are different aspects of grown-up amusement that the two people appreciate, notwithstanding the self-evident vaginal infiltration. A portion of these are various types of genuine demonstration itself, and some are more pre-sex customs that can be viewed as various types of foreplay. This is similarly as significant (if not more significant) than realizing the correct comments or wear to turn on your mate.

Foreplay

We'll go through a couple of models here to know about when learning your new mate or spicing things up with your present playmate.

Pornography: This is something that must be taken care of carefully, as there are various kinds of erotic entertainment, and not all things are for each crowd. For instance, your mate might be exceptionally intrigued by man-on-man grown-up acts; however, you may have some private matters with watching this sort of activity occur, whether strict or individual untouchable. In the event that this was the situation, you have to voice your interests. There are more dubious kinds of sexual entertainment, for example, assault pornography, and this makes the vast majority awkward. If this somehow managed to come up, understand what you will say and how you will respond. However, perhaps he's not into erotic entertainment, or you share a similar classification of interest when seeing grown-up recordings - at that point, all frameworks go! Continuously trust your gut impulses and never watch or take part in something that causes you to feel less sexual.

Substantial petting: This one is a touch more self-evident, open, and you probably have no issues in this division. There are erogenous zones that are comparative from individual to individual, and you can unquestionably begin here while investigating your mate's body. However, they may have different regions that get their engine running quicker than the conventional spots. This could be their neck.

If so, some light kissing and licking will drive them wild. It very well may be their upper thigh. This interest makes for a lot simpler change into kicking the large things off also. You can never turn out badly by asking your man where he needs to be contacted - there's nothing more sizzling than being the chief.

Dress up play: This could resemble a combination of things. Also, what could be more amusing to add some extra hotness to the blend? You can be anything you need to be, and a more certain you also. Perhaps he enjoys more dream type situations, leaving you to choices of taking on the appearance of goddesses or anecdotal computer game characters. Maybe he's more into the conventional provocative jobs, so you can be an attractive attendant, a horny artist, or a mischievous student. He's most probably open to a recommendation, as long as your pussy is available and boobies are out. Make a round of it! At some point, you're the instructor, and you're here to direct train. Another you're his devoted attendant, helping to all his necessities. This additionally offers him the chance to change his jobs and practice his hand at realizing what you like also. It's a positive, mutually advantageous arrangement, and nothing is more enjoyable.

You most likely knew this was coming. This could be an exceptionally advising and off-kilter part of becoming more acquainted with one another; that is the direst outcome imaginable, however. Without a doubt, regardless of what is emerging from your storage room (in a real sense), he will be absolutely into it. Among probably the most well-known obsessions are simply the classifications joy (masturbation) or watching another person jerk off. However long you're not pulling out a twofold sided dildo that you're hoping to impart to your man, he most likely won't be exceptionally frightened or awkward. He might be more modest and awkward to share any toys that he has with you. However, he may have a few. So, you should be ready for that. In spite of the fact that a few men utilize some kind of vibrator to invigorate themselves anally, almost certainly, he has utilized such a cock sock or pocket pussy. You can participate in this sort of grown-up fun, too! Get inventive! Utilize your creative mind! This is what is the issue here. Additional fun: food in the room. Of course, he's beefcake, and you look adequate to eat, yet getting substantial, consumable food is such a flavorful method to "zest" or "improve" things up, in a manner of speaking. You can utilize whipped garnish and press it out onto his "part," so you can draw it off, or you can trickle liquefied chocolate everywhere on your body, driving down to your woman pieces and let him lick you here and there. In the event that both of you are somewhat more diverse and carefree, something intriguing like laying pepperonis in innovative spots on your body might be something that suits both of you somewhat more suitably. Whatever works for both of you, let it all out. Maybe food isn't generally your flavor in the room, and that is fine as well.

We've talked dirty, then...

Presently comes genuine fun! Sex is a delightful, cozy act that unites two individuals in an incredible manner; this doesn't mean it must be not kidding or need fun! There are various approaches to begin into the 'dirty-dirty,' and each couple is extraordinary and appreciates various things. Usually, the man and lady substitute performing oral sex on one another; either bringing each other to peak or in a prodding way. Here is an incredible spot to enter a portion of the more innovative expressions you learned before!

In the event that you are attempting to get him exasperated up, yet without debilitating his part, avoid the "completing moves," like stating anything identified with needing him to cum or needing his swimmers in your mouth. That is giving the green light, which could leave you unsatisfied on the off chance that you were anticipating vaginal intercourse. A decent heading to go is talking about how horny he makes you or how wet you are. This could seem like, "I've been pondering your dick throughout the day" or "I am so amazing wet at the present time."

Talking about how wet your pussy is will make him consider dropping your underwear and giving you the D in a significant manner. Be that as it may, in the event that you truly simply need to satisfy him orally and perhaps receive some head consequently, don't hesitate to hit with certain expressions more like, "You better cum for me," or "I can hardly wait to taste you climax." Then it is all frameworks go! Presently, don't be hesitant to request what you need! Numerous ladies are so humiliated to request their man to go down on them or contact them in a manner that is satisfying. Trust me here: he needs to lick and contact you.

There is no greater turn-on than making a lady arrive at a climax; this is for a couple of reasons. Initial, a lady's climax is a wonderful, grand second, and it's overly provocative. Furthermore, he needs to feel your fascination in him in an actual indication. He may know you're into him, particularly when you're talking dirty, yet this really shows exactly how into him that you are. Lastly, it causes him to

feel amazing. He's the man. He's your man.
Also, presently he'll feel like it.

Headstrong period

You've developed one another while talking
dirty throughout the day, you've probably
worn a coordinating bra and undies set to
set the temperament, you've participated in
various pre-sexual acts to turn out to be
significantly more private, and you've got each
other off. You're in the hard-headed period.
You're depleted, likely ravenous, parched, and
you're prepared for a shower. The closeness
doesn't need to end! Perhaps the greatest error
that a couple can make is to complete personal
occasions after you've cum.

Hit the shower together! While you may wind
up beginning the entire cycle once more, it
is attractive and happy with things to have
the option to shower together and wash each

other up! Spurt the cleanser and cleanser on one another, flush each other off, and alternate drying each other down. Slip-on his shirt after you're completely gotten dry to give him that "she's mine" feeling. Let him feel like he claims you. You're his property now.

One of you snatches some food, while the different gets a few beverages. Perhaps you're an espresso kind of couple, or possibly you appreciate mixed drinks in the wake of doing the enormous detonation; whatever works for you! The key here is functioning as a group to address each other's issues. In case you're actually feeling extra soft emotional, you can share a plate or feed one another. Get re-energized together so you can deplete each other again in a short time. Rests together and get some rest.

Perhaps it's the center of your Saturday, and it's not exactly sleeping time. Turn on Netflix and unwind while marathon watching your number one sitcoms or professional comics. Turn on a portion of your #1 quieting music. Simply ingest one another and be each other's solace. Whenever you're refreshed up and re-powered, possibly begin utilizing your dirty talk once more. "I can't quit contemplating how you felt within me," or "Gosh, I can hardly wait to screw you once more." It won't be long until his juices are streaming again, and his little officers are blasting to attack your space.

Chapter 2

Types of dirty talk with examples

B esides the way that it feels so damn great, sex talk is an extraordinary device to construct strain. In the event that you attempt it, you will love it, and your sexual coexistence will be better than anyone might have expected—that I exclusively guarantee. In any case, before you decide to dirty talk to somebody, you need to choose what sort of dirty talk you will utilize:

• Soft dirty talk

• Slowly arriving dirty talk

- Hardcore dirty talk

You can utilize delicate dirty talk as a method for being a tease when you just met the person, and perhaps you need something else.

It's an incredibly blameless sort of dirty talk, likewise extraordinary for fledglings.

Instances of Delicate Dirty Talk

Come sit on my lap, love.

Damn, you smell sufficiently pleasant to eat.

Do you think I have undies at this moment?

Feeling you on top of me and in control is the most sultry thing ever!

I can hardly wait to be separated from everyone else with you.

I can hardly wait to have you inside me. /I can hardly wait to be inside you.

I can hardly wait to taste you all the rage.

I could go the entire day between your legs.

I feel so powerless and turned on simultaneously when I'm in your arms.

I get so turned on, contemplating the last time we had intercourse.

I love it when you snarl.

I love the amazing way you take a gander at me when we're together; it's so hot!

I love the way you take a gander at me when you're turned on.

I love the wonderful way your hands feel on me.

I love it when you talk to me like that.

I need to give you the best oral sex you've ever had.

I need to tie you up later and have my way with you.

I need you at the present time.

I need you to gradually kiss me from my lips, down my neck, onto my bosoms, and right down my body.

I need you to prod me until I can take it no more.

I simply need to be utilized by you today around evening time. Would I be able to be your own toy?

I simply need to make your entire face wet with my juices.

I was considering you the previous evening before I rested.

I'm getting so turned on/wet/hard.

In the event that you continue taking a gander at me that way, I'm not liable for what befalls your cock.

Is it accurate to say that you are an eager child? I need to gobble you up.

Mmm... I can tell that you're having a great time.

Mmm... treat you so harshly as that?

On the off chance that we weren't here, in (embed public spot) at the present time, you'd have definitely zero chance of keeping your garments on.

Simply lie back and let me deal with you.

Simply stand by till we return home...

That feels stunning, infant.

Think about what I'm wearing under this.

Ughhh... I love your body to such an extent.

What are you accomplishing after work? I need a portion of your cock ASAP.

What do you want to do to me?

You feel so great within my infant.

You get me so hot.

You look so excellent/attractive/ravishing/masculine at this moment.

You look so screwing great! I can hardly wait to get you home.

The second sort of dirty talk is extraordinary to utilize when you didn't choose yet on which level of dirty talking you need. Simply go with it, and meanwhile, you'll choose what type is ideal for the circumstance.

Chapter 3

Instances of 'Gradually Arriving' Dirty Talk

(Grasping her hand and putting it over her vagina) Show me how you contact yourself infant... I need to see you giving up into your most profound joy for me.

At the point when you pull my hair, it makes me need to come.

Continuing onward, continue onward!

Cum in my mouth. I need to taste you.

Do anything you desire with me, daddy.

I love feeling you in my grasp!

I love it when I can press my pussy around your cock.

I love the way you taste.

I need to rule you today around evening time.

I need you right inside me; give me every one of you.

I need you to assume responsibility for me.

I need you to be as uproarious as you can when you come.

I need you to complete any place you like.

I need you to cum all over me.

I need you to cum for me.

I need you to cum within me.

I need you to screw me before the mirror infant.

I never need you to stop, it feels so great.

I will deplete every single ounce of cum out of you.

In that general area!

Is this pussy yours? Is it true that you will take it?

Jump on your knees, presently.

Mmm... I screwing love it when I ride you like this.

More profound/harder/quicker.

Pound my little pussy with your large cock daddy.

Request consent before you cum... I need to hear you ask for it.

Reveal to me the amount you love it when I screw you/when you screw me.

Simply lie back and let me get it done.

Try not to stop!

Unwind... simply lie back and let me make you cum.

You are a decent little prostitute, right?

You have a skilled mouth.

You have such an ideal cock... I love it to such an extent.

You have such an ideal/beautiful cock... I love it to such an extent.

You look so screwing attractive at this moment.

You ruling me is such a turn on.

You seem as though an attractive darling with your lips folded over me like this.

You will fail to remember your name after I'm finished screwing you today.

Your cock fits in me so consummately.

Your cock is so heavenly.

Then again, there is an in-your-face dirty talk. This is more for the geniuses and the individuals who have been seeing someone some time, so they really understand what their mate likes and how he will respond.

Instances of In-Your-Face Dirty Talk

At the point when you hold my bum that way, It causes me to detonate.

Disclose to me how severely you need me to screw you.

For what reason wouldn't i be able to have you like this constantly? You're my new compulsion.

his cock is all I require—and perhaps some air.

How would you need me to screw you? Like this?

I believe I'm infatuated with your dick.

I love being your screw prostitute.

I love it when you crush your cock into me.

I love sucking your cock, daddy.

I need to feel you shoot your heap in my mouth.

I need to feel your cum everywhere all over.

I need you to screw me until we awaken the neighbors.

I'm your prostitute.

Indeed, that is the thing that I like. That is so hot. Screw me more.

Keep that pretty little mouth open to me when I'm screwing it.

Let me jump on top of your cock, darling.

Mmmmm... definitely, screw my face.

My goodness, I'm cumming.

No doubt daddy, give me each and every drop of your delectable cum.

No doubt, ruin my pussy. Take it!

Pound me harder!

Reveal to me who possesses this screwing pussy?

Screw me hard.

Slow and simple, or quick and insane. I'll screw you anyway you like.

Snatch my hair and screw me like a canine.

Stand up and screw me.

That pretty little face has the right to get screwed.

Try not to make a sound until I advise you to... and in the event that you do, I will respite and stand by until you can hush up once more, similar to a decent young man/young lady.

Use me like your little screw toy.

We should fuck once more. I need more.

What a polite little prostitute you are.

What devious easily overlooked detail do you need me to do to you next?

Would you like to watch me suck you?

You cause me so wet it doesn't to feel genuine.

You have no clue about what you've gotten yourself into. I will be your sex slave.

You have to snatch my tits and hold them while I cum.

You will make me drop with joy.

You will require supports when I'm finished screwing you.

Your cock is gigantic.

Your dick is so full. It feels stunning.

When to use dirty talk with examples

Sexting:

Sexting can go from delicate dirty talking to truly no-nonsense. It relies upon which heading you need to take it. Normally, sexting the most secure approach since you have a ton of time to consider what you will send, and you don't need to be worried you will make a simpleton out of yourself. The danger of humiliating yourself is insignificant.

Here are a few writings you can utilize, contingent upon the circumstance you're in:

Anticipating having you later.

At whatever point your name springs up on my screen, my knees debilitate.

Considering you contacting me, in a real sense, it turns me on.

Disclose to me your mystery obsession. I wager I'll like it.

Guess what? I need to feel you so terrible at this point.

I believe it's time we attempted (fill in the clear).

I don't get it how it happens without fail, yet the second you lick my areolas, my legs get powerless.

I get excited with energy when your fingers dance on my wet floor.

I had so many dirty musings today... Guess who propelled them all?

I have a mystery – I'm viewing an exceptionally dirty video online at this moment...

I have a secret for you, yet I'll provide you some insight. This evening, I'm going to make you the extraordinary visitor between my legs.

I just escaped a hot shower. I'm drenching wet at this moment.

I need to perceive how great your tongue can play between my holes.

I was contemplating you and me and abruptly, suddenly, I wound up totally stripped and wet down under. How could that occur?!

I was taking a gander at the sex toys today.

I would prefer to be sleeping with you. At the present time.

I'll be wearing just heels this evening...

I'm composing this with one hand in light of the fact that my other hand is occupied...

I'm contacting myself. Really awful you're not here.

I'm envisioning your hands on my body... your mouth on my body... lastly, your body on mine.

I'm so bashful, yet you have no clue about I'm's opinion.

I'm under endless covers I'm as yet cool... I surmise I should get into some garments...

In the event that we were together, what might you need me to do to you?

Infant, you are excessively hot for me to stand up to.

It causes me to feel incredibly hot when you contact me down there.

It sounds abnormal; however, I was unable to prevent myself from contemplating us the previous evening. I play it again and again in my brain, and it feels sooo great.

Lying in bed and exhausted. Wish you were here to play Simon Says with me.

My flat mate is away for the end of the week. We can be as uproarious as we need, and I am anticipating destroying the dividers.

Next time I see you, I need to be as dirty as could be expected under the circumstances.

Pause, are only you at this moment.

Send me your nudes, and I'll send you mine.

Simply needed to reveal to you that my new red clothing feels great and attractive on my skin. I could show it to you in the event that you were here at this point.

Simply needing to tell you that I'm lying on my bed bare considering you.

The considerations I was having about you were dirty to such an extent that I needed to clean up.

This new clothing feels soooo great against my skin...

Today around evening time I need you to disrobe me gradually with your strong touch and nibble every last bit of my body with no inch left immaculate.

We should make one thing straight. At the point when we meet later on, there will be no foreplay.

What are you wearing at this moment? I trust you don't utter a word!

Would you be able to figure the shade of my underwear? On the off chance that you get it right, I will give you anything you need today.

You were shouting some smudged words the previous evening. Wanna do it again this evening?

Chapter 4

Dirty inquiries:

Dirty talk can be utilized in all assortments, so they go a long way past provocative writings. Shouldn't something be said about inquiries? Have you ever thought about how to talk dirty to a person utilizing questions that will stir him, constructing the shared sexual pressure and turning him on like nobody could possibly do previously?

Do you lean toward your lady shaved or all regular?

Do you like me on top or on the base?

Do you like sexting?

Do you like the lights on or off?

Do you like watching me contact myself?

Do you need me to talk dirty?

Do you want to be in charge or you'd like me to take the wheel?

Does the idea of recording a video turn you on?

Harsh or exotic?

Have you ever attempted eatable clothing?

Have you ever been discovered going performance?

Have you ever dated two young ladies simultaneously?

Have you ever done it before others?

Have you ever done it in the water?

Have you ever engaged in sexual relations in broad daylight?

Have you ever envisioned about me?

Have you ever had a trio?

Have you ever had butt-centric sex? What's your opinion about it?

Have you ever played strip poker?

Have you ever utilized an ointment?

Have you ever utilized food while you're doing it?

Have you ever utilized sex toys?

I rest exposed; isn't that right?

Is it accurate to say that you are a boob fellow or a butt fellow?

Okay actually do it in a vehicle?

Okay prefer to play dirty Truth or Dare?

Think about what I'm wearing at this moment?

What do you figure I should wear to bed?

What do you think my lips taste like?

What is the naughtiest thing you've ever done?

What is your #1 part of my body?

What is your greatest sex dream?

What might you do in the event that I send you a dirty photograph of me?

What might you do on the off chance that I addressed the entryway bare?

What sort of outfit might you want to see me in?

What's the longest you've abandoned doing it?

What's your #1 position?

Where is the naughtiest spot that you've done it?

Where would you like to contact me at the present time?

Would you be able to figure the shade of the clothing I'm wearing at the present time?

Dirty foreplay talk:

Foreplay is the main piece of the entire sex act, and in the event that you take care of business, you'll certainly have the best sex of your life.

Alright, angel, you can have any opening you need.

At the point when we return home, I will make you climax so hard.

Chomp me, and make me yours.

Chomp me.

Come for me.

Come here and ride me hard!

Cum for me infant, cum in my mouth, I need to taste you.

Cum for me.

Debase me.

Did you take a seminar on the best way to make me come?

Do you like it when I contact myself here?

Do you like my succulent pussy/enormous dick? Mention to me what you see. Depict it to me.

Do you need more? Take it!

Don't you try to come until I state you can!

Fuck.

Get here, enormous kid. Also, exercise authority over me!

Get here.

Get my butt.

Give me that come, nectar. I need it in my mouth. Please, offer it to me.

Gracious, infant, that was the best screw I've ever had. Much obliged to you for that. Phrases to say during intercourse

Groan for me.

Harder.

Hold me.

I can scarcely focus; I simply continue considering you snatching me and taking me.

I can't accept what you're doing! Kindly don't stop!

I could go through hours between your legs; prodding... sucking; tasting; tasting you.

I don't have any underwear on.

I feel so horny and vulnerable when you overwhelm me

I feel so mind blowing when you press your penis against me.

I generally get what I need.

I have an attractive astonishment for you later...
x

I have to feel you against me.

I have to feel you inside me.

I longed for you the previous evening and woke up dribbling wet—basically like at this moment.

I love grasping your cock and feeling it getting hard.

I love it when you coarseness your teeth.

I love it when you contact me there.

I love it when you give me 'the look'.

I love it when you murmur in my ear.

I love it when you screw me like a whore.

I love it when you wear tight garments.

I love it when you're harsh with me.

I love satisfying you and the hints of your pleasure make me insane.

I love sucking your cock. What's more, I will lick it clean.

I love the delightful way hard you can make me come.

I love the manner in which it sounds when you screw me. Hear it?

I love the manner in which you groan.

I love the manner in which you taste.

I love the manner in which you top me off.

I love the way enormous your cock gets when I talk to you like this.

I love your body.

I love your dick.

I need it all over me. Cover me with it.

I need to feel your cock in my mouth.

I need to hear you shout my name when you cum.

I need to nod off with you inside me.

I need to see you play with yourself.

I need to taste you.

I need to taste your cum.

I need you between my thighs.

I need you in me so baaadly.

I need you to cuff me and screw me any way you'd like.

I need you to kiss my whole body.

I need you to screw me from behind.

I need you to shout my name when you come.

I need you to strip me.

I need you to suck out all the juices you put in me with your mouth.

I need you to take me in your arms and make me cum hard.

I need you to tie me up.

I need you to uncover and hang tight for me in the room.

I need you within me.

I need you. I need to have intercourse with you. I need to appreciate sex with you. I need to screw you.

I need your cock in my mouth.

I need your cum.

I need your lips against my skin.

I need your mouth on me.

I simply need to be your little screw doll...

I simply need to fold my pussy over your cock.

I totally love feeling you on top of me.

I will break you this evening

I will deplete your balls this evening!

I will do you at this moment, nectar. Your pussy... or your butt...?

I will make you cry with joy.

I will make you shout and ask for additional.

I will make you shout constantly today!

I will require some boss adjusting in the following ten minutes.

I will stamp you as mine today around evening time.

I wish I could control myself better around you, yet when I see you, all I need to do is rip your garments off and screw you.

I wish we could simply remain in bed and have intercourse the entire day – Perfect when he is leaving your place to keep the sexual strain high.

I wore this underwear only for you.

I would prefer not to feel my face or hands after you're finished with me.

I would prefer not to have the option to walk tomorrow so screw me harder.

If it's not too much trouble

If it's not too much trouble screw me harder daddy.

I'm so fuckin' wet, just let me suck your sweet candy...

I'm so wet/extreme at this moment.

I'm trickling.

I'm wanting you.

I'm your slave for the evening. Mention to me what you need.

In any event, when you're feeling terrible, I need to screw you.

In that general area.

In the event that these individuals weren't here, I would be on my knees with your cock in my mouth.

In the event that we weren't at this gathering and these individuals weren't anywhere near, I would bounce you at the present time!

Infant don't stop! Goodness my god, I love it when you do that!

It makes me insane when you take a gander at me that way.

It may sound ravenous, yet I need your cock so terrible at this moment.

It's a pity we're not in bed right now since everything I can consider is feeling your body on mine.

I've been a trouble maker, and I merit a hitting.

I've been truly downright awful should be rebuffed.

I've never been fulfilled that way.

I've never been kissed that way.

Jump on all fours, darling... and stand by like a decent young lady.

Kiss me there... Lick every last bit of me.

Kiss my areolas.

Lie back and shut up! I will make you come until you can't relax.

Make me cum with your tongue.

Make me your bitch!

Make me your bitch.

Making you cum hard is my main need at the present time.

Making you hard is my main need.

More profound! (at that point, pull him more profound with your arms and legs)

More profound.

More slow.

More.

Much the same as that.

Murmur in my ear.

No one has ever screwed me as you do.

No stops this time. How about we perceive how often I can make you come.

Okay discipline me in the event that I was acting bratty?

On the off chance that you do your best, you have some joy/fun coming your direction.

Play with my clit.

Possibly you should hit me – I've been incredibly, awful.

Pull my hair and slap me.

Pull my hair.

Put your infant creator inside my opening and screw my cerebrum out!

Put your mouth on my bosoms.

Quicker! More profound! Harder!

Quicker.

Quiet the fuck down! I'll screw you any place I need, mischievous little prostitute!

Quiet the fuck down, and remove my garments immediately.

Quit seeing me like that, it's making me wet.

Realizing that you can totally overwhelm me makes me so insane horny

Rebuff me; I've been insidious.

Reveal to me all the dirty seemingly insignificant details you do when you jerk off, you devious kid/young lady. Disclose to me everything, child. Reveal to me how you play with yourself.

Screw me harder.

Screw me like you own me.

Screw me like you would not joke about this!

Screw me. At the present time!

Screw my cunt.

Simply get my head and power me closer!

Simply stand by until we return home.

Slap my butt!

Snatch my bosoms and press my areolas.

Spread your legs wide for me, sweet dear. Your body is mine today around evening time.

State my name.

Stifle me.

Stroke my cock.

Stronger.

Suck my areolas until I state it's sufficient.

Take a gander at me.

Take me on the spot.

Take your garments off, and get your hands on my knees. At this moment!!

Talk to me.

Taste me.

That was mind boggling.

Think about what shading my undies are?

To manufacture expectation:

Today around evening time we will would what I like to do. In any case, don't stress, it will be loads of fun!

Today will be loads of fun

Top me off with bliss.

Top me off, daddy, screw my tight cunt! Make me shout with that large dick of yours!

Top me off.

Touch me all finished.

Touch yourself and let me watch you.

Try not to stop.

Try not to stop.

Use me as your toy throughout the night.

Use me.

We have to meet after work; this horniness is slaughtering me.

What a hot frightful young lady you are! I will clean your mouth out with my cum in the event that you talk dirty, underhanded young lady.

What a sweet hot ass!

What might you incline toward I wear today, a strap or undies or nothing by any means?

What might you say on the off chance that I requested that you go down on me at the present time?

Where would you like to come?

You can have me any way you need...

You do that so well.

You feel so great inside me.

You like how I screw you?

You like it when I spread my legs and take you in?

You like that?

You look so screwing sweltering toward the beginning of the day.

You need to go once more?

You whore, I will screw you till you can't walk! Are you game?

You will make me cum.

You won't have the option to walk tomorrow.

Your cock/pussy feels stunning.

Your tongue is mystical.

You're my bitch. I venerate how mischievous you are. I love you.

You're not leaving here until I have your cum in my mouth.

Others are...

1. I will make you shout as I did last time

Telling your lady how you will make her insane in bed simply like the last time is sufficient to turn her on. The memory is sufficient to make her insane. Thus, when you begin making out, murmur this into her ears and stick consistent with your words. Make her shout and make it vital for her.

2. I will kiss you where you need me to

You need to state this just in the event that you would not joke about this. Show your lady that you care about her pleasure as well and in this manner, you will successfully give her that. Kiss her any place she needs to on the grounds that she will cherish your consideration. This will likewise give her a sentiment of being in charge and completing things her way.

3. You have such a hot (your #1 body part)

This should be told when you are having intercourse since that is the point at which the effect is more. During sex, disclose to her that you locate a specific body part exceptionally hot. Saying it when you are contacting that part and feeling it is the thing that makes it so hot. It will turn her on and furthermore cause her to feel exceptionally positive about bed.

4. I love it when you groan

Telling your lady that you love it when she groans implies you love it when you watch her appreciate sex. Truth be told she may groan somewhat more simply because she realizes you love it and that is pleasurable for you two.

5. You make me hot when you (her #1 move that you love)

Another extremely hot thing to tell your lady in bed is You make me hot when you contact me down there. The entire aim here is to turn her on and add some flavor to sex. At the point when you mention to your better half what you love the most in bed, it is likewise a method of uncovering what you like in bed. Ladies love to hear their mates do the dirty talk in bed since that keeps them sure and they won't be off-kilter during sex.

6. I will go in more profound

Ladies who appreciate sex will cherish it when they will hear this. Simply state, I will go further and harder and her groans will make you all insane. Hold her tight and just before you are going to enter; say this investigating her eyes. Also, as you state it, enter her gradually and increment the movement.

Aside from these you can likewise talk about your sexual dreams during sex. Nonetheless, it must be kept to one sentence. For example, you can advise her, I need to have intercourse with you in a shower. Such talks during sex will simply improve it for both of you in bed.

Chapter 5

After Sex:

Dirty talk isn't just for the room. Here's some motivation for dirty comments to your mate to keep sexual energy streaming in your relationship.

As yet feeling sore after the previous evening

At the point when you arrive, I'm going to [sexual activity].

Here and there my legs get powerless when you kiss me.

I believe you're the main person who can drive me crazy and horny simultaneously.

I can hardly wait to screw you today.

I can in any case taste you.

I can't get you crazy.

I continue considering your body against mine.

I feel so little when you fold your arms over me... I miss this to such an extent.

I jerked off about you the previous evening. – Learn incredible masturbation methods here and considerably more here.

I know it's been a difficult day. That is the reason I'm going to [insert sexual activity] when you return home.

I miss your cock.

I need to be your woman in the city and your oddity between the sheets.

I need you so terrible.

I never figured I would meet somebody that gets me so god dam excited.

I should be working; however, everything I can consider is you overwhelming me.

I truly preferred it when we [insert sexual activity]. How about we attempt that once more.

In the event that we could just engage in sexual relations in a single situation for the remainder of our lives, what might it be?

It makes me horny when you [fill in the blank].

I've been anticipating sitting all over the entire day.

I've been pondering [fill in the blank] the entire day, and I can hardly wait until we can [fill in the blank].

Likely arrangements:

My body misses your [insert body part].

Perceptions:

Pondering you makes me need to contact myself.

Recall the previous evening when we [insert sexual activity]? Goodness.

Recollections:

Simply contemplating you makes me so dam wet

That thing you do with your [insert body part] truly makes me hot.

The sultriest thing about the previous evening was feeling you shoot your heap inside me.

What sex position was your top pick?

What's your opinion about doing [insert sexual activity] whenever we're sleeping?

You look sufficient to place in my mouth today.

You make me so wet/hard when you groan.

You're generally at the forefront of my thoughts.

The Most Effective Method to Talk Dirty on Telephone

Regardless of whether you're having telephone sex unexpectedly or you're in a significant distance relationship, here are some dirty comments when you're essentially interfacing with somebody. Customize these expressions to accommodate your relationship, and match the language you and your mate as of now use. Keep in mind, one couple's vanilla is another couple's wrinkle.

Get into it gradually

Allow yourself to go at your own movement. Sharing your dreams through content might be a superior decision in case you're not happy with any up close and personal play yet. You're on no one's timetable to figure out how to dirty talk aside from your own. (Here's our full manual for sexting, in the event that you're interested.)

Don't think too much.

It doesn't need to be very innovative, yet it should feel great to you and your mate. Great sex should free and explorative. The dirty things you state to your mate should feel characteristic and stream with the occasion.

Have a great time.

Let dirty talk lift your sexual experience, not frustrate it. The sooner you dismiss the weight you put on yourself, the simpler investigating the sexual experience will be. You can enable your mate to explore your body. Shoot, it might even prompt all the more satisfying sex for everybody included.

Stay away from points of interest.

At the point when you need to portray the second for your mate, you don't need to specify their size or their circumference. Something as straightforward as "I love your body" can get the show on the road. Also, in the event that you need to toss in a couple of descriptive words, officers like—fat, tremendous, and wet function admirably.

Get settled with your mate.

The solace you feel in your relationship has an inseparable tie to what you're willing to attempt explicitly. Talking with your partner(s) in advance about your inclinations in dirty talk can be an incredible method to decrease the tension when you're really at the time. Convey, investigate, and impart some more.

Forgo judging.

A more prominent feeling of closeness can bloom in your relationship by figuring out how to talk dirty. Dirty talking isn't about it being gross or unrefined or foul. It's only more about, does it cause you to feel hot? What makes an expression dirty is the way explicitly stirred you get from hearing it. Be the individual that champions somebody's sexual dream, not pounds it.

Phrases for when you are longing

At the point when I get back, I'm going to [insert sexual activity].

Do you miss my body?

I can hardly wait until I can go down on you once more.

I love it when you talk that way.

I miss the manner in which you feel within me.

I miss the manner in which you taste.

I miss the way your [insert body part] feels [insert verb] against my [insert body part].

I need to feel how wet/hard you are.

I need to see you naked...right now.

I want to be there.

I will screw you so hard when I see you.

I wish I could hold you at the present time.

I'll rip your garments off the second I see you.

I'm contacting myself. Would you like to taste?

In the mind-set:

Inquiries for recess:

Is it accurate to say that you are contacting yourself?

Is it accurate to say that you are distant from everyone else?

Mention to me what you need from me.

Mention to me what you need to do to me.

Murmur dirty things to me.

Play with yourself for me.

Pondering you is making me so wet/extreme at the present time.

Simply hearing your voice makes me need to contact myself

The way you're sexting me is hot; need to show me what you're talking about?

What are you wearing at the present time?

What else do you like when I do it to you?

Would you like to have FaceTime sex?

Would you like to hear me out come?

Phrases to Say During Orgasm

As should be obvious, you have countless approaches to talk dirty to somebody and make them accused of sexual pressure. A portion of these are pretty in-your-face, yet some are totally honest—it depends what you like and in what direction you need to go. The fact is that anybody can dirty talk.

You simply need to dispose of the blockage in your psyche and lift yourself up with certainty since when you consider it, it's truly not so troublesome. In the event that you don't have the foggiest idea what to state or your dread is hindering you from totally unwinding, attempt a portion of the proposals above, just to have something to begin with.

When you slacken up totally, you'll disregard what you do and don't need to state, and it will just emerge from your mouth—making your mate unfathomably horny. He will thank you later for getting a climax he will always remember. That is what amount dirty talking can be amazing. Attempt it, don't be bashful!

Chapter 6

Things to never say

I'm a firm devotee to talking dirty in bed. It's fun, energizing, thoroughly stimulating, and truly improves the experience. It's additionally simply one more type of correspondence, which all closeness requires; however, the sort of correspondence that is more about hot stuff than the capable stuff. Obviously, you need to impart about contraception and insurance; however, then once the garments are off, you need to get down to the great stuff.

You could be an absolute dynamo or a sourpuss in bed, in any case, sex can once in a while be requesting and befuddling. In the event that you've been with your mate over a genuinely significant stretch of time, you're presumably in-a state of harmony with what he loves, what you like and the works.

Nonetheless, in case you're in a generally new relationship and have not yet investigated each other's sexual ideals and indecencies, this article may come convenient. Presently everybody has an alternate kind of sex drive, and sorting out your mate's sort will make your life a ton simpler and your sex a ton better. And keeping in mind that that entire cycle may take some time, here's some guidance on where you can begin...

Talking during sex isn't some tea, yet in case you're the sort who appreciates it and needs to start it to try things out, ensure you understand what you're doing. Now and again it doesn't take a lot to turn somebody off, particularly in case you're proclaiming things that distract him. In case you will go there – do it well.

I'm about legit correspondence in the room. In any case, there's a distinction between being straightforward and saying each and every thing that strikes a chord. There are a few things you should just never say in bed under any conditions, in light of the fact that as opposed to getting your mate in the mind-set, you'll just lead them to close down.

On the off chance that you need to turn out to be more informative in the room, there are a lot of things you can say. "What improve, this or this?", "Treat you so harshly as that?", "I like that," and "That feels so great" are for the most part extraordinary spots to begin. In the event that you will probably give criticism, there's a careful method to do that, as well. Take a stab at beginning with something you love about your sexual coexistence, at that point, requesting something new and repeating the positive once more. "Guide them and give consolation when they hit a spot you like." That way, your mate won't be left inclination unreliable.

Dirty talk can likewise be fun, yet examine it ahead of time to ensure you're just making statements your mate really needs to hear. Discover a chance to talk about it outside the warmth existing apart from everything else, and clarify what you do need and what you don't need also.

There are a few expressions, nonetheless, that are probably going to leave your mate feeling uncertain, forced, or upset. Here are a few things you ought to likely try not to state in bed.

However, the thing with talking dirty is that, despite the fact that it's a complete impact particularly once you get its hang, there is a "right" and "wrong" approach to do it. I don't intend to give anybody a complex; however, actually when you're amidst talking dirty with your mate, there's simply a few things you shouldn't specify. Here are those things you ought to never say during dirty talk in bed.

Try not to talk too much

Regardless of whether what your mate just said is very hot so your cerebrum goes into the heading of, "I need to state that, as well," simply don't do it. You need to have a dirty exchange not somebody surrendering the dirty merchandise while you rehash what they just said. On the off chance that you're so motivated by what they needed to state, at that point, change it a piece.

Regardless of whether you're somebody who cherishes a babble, presently isn't an ideal opportunity to talk about their mum, whether the clothing needs doing or how that work meeting went. Clearly, it's generally evident to a great many people that sex isn't a chance to get up to speed; however, it took me some time to discover that.

Don't mention babies

You could have had the conversation about making a baby before starting out, but try not to mention babies during sex. It could be a turnoff for some people, and it could even scare others off if it's completely new to them. If the thought comes to you during sex, hold it off till you're done.

Cutoff references about food

Truly, in an ideal world food and closeness ought to go inseparably; however, that doesn't mean your dirty talk is the best spot for it. For instance, screaming zucchini, pickle or wiener may make you both hungry. That is in addition to being a diversion to the whole process.

Being too sweet is a bad idea

"Love making" or "having intercourse" aren't too bad expressions, but they have a tone to them that does not go too well with dirty talk. Therefore, for dirty talk to strike the perfect chords, you might want to reconsider being too sweet. Of course, making love with or screwing are still very valid on their own as far as love is concerned. So, lay off being too delicate with your words when talking dirty; you need to get your mate worked up, not prep them for a sentimental tryst in an air pocket shower encompassed by candles.

There should be no mention of your ex

This does not need too much explanation. Brining in the name of your ex is like flipping a switch that urns your partner down immediately. Plus, it sends too many wrong questions. Your partner does not need to how he's doing compared to your former lover either. Compliment your man or woman as much as you want, but do not bring in a name from somewhere.

Try not to contrast or balance your band together with any other person. It'll just cause them to feel deficient or envious. On the off chance that you need them to accomplish something the manner in which your ex did it, simply request that thing legitimately. Furthermore, don't anticipate that they should like what your ex did; everybody's unique.

Think again about being freaky

Unusual and freaky can be truly extraordinary!
Yet, just in case you're on the same wavelength.
In the event that you begin murmuring in your
mate's ear that you need to see them tied
up, bound, and fixed by the person who lives
nearby, the state of mind will be demolished,
particularly if your mate wants to try fixing
out.

Do not make body references that are weird

Knowing how to mention body parts is a
skill you must possess to pull off this whole
dirty talk scene. Mention them, but make
sure it is not weird. Obviously, you can
praise your mate's body; however, remarks
about appearance can get touchy. Ensure your
assertions fall off sure, not equivocal. Try not to
tell somebody they make amusing or odd faces
or commotions, regardless of whether you
mean it positively. Also, don't make reference

to the size or state of a body part — trying to say that you love it or it's ideal is sufficient.

Abstain from creating complicated scenarios

The thing with talking dirty is you need to remain at the time. Obviously thinking of situations is truly alluring yet you would prefer not to make a situation that is excessively convoluted. You need to keep it at any rate fairly substantial in nature. Dirty talk shouldn't include contemplating too much that it takes your mind off the most important thing at the moment.

You're not hard enough

We've all been there. It's simply not going in and you both know why. In this off-kilter situation, every so often, an innocent exaggeration is in order. Simply imagine it doesn't fit, it's simpler along these lines and nobody's emotions get injured.

Are you coming?

Otherwise known as, "Are you almost done?"
You might have orgasmed earlier, or possibly
you're simply getting a piece sleepy and
hungry. In any case, pressure is no-one's
companion in the room. Take a stab at
exchanging up positions to suit you, or
unpretentiously asking, "is there anything you
need me to do?" Or, you know, simply be
straightforward and state you're not feeling it.

I did not fart

For what reason do certain sex positions
make clamors that sound embarrassingly like
fart? Anyway, as embarrassing this might be,
simply have a giggle and proceed onward. It's
absolutely typical. Try not to do what some
would do by making up ridiculous excuses.

"More, more, more"

He's as of now putting forth a valiant effort so don't request more when he can't give it. This applies to screaming too much "harder." Also, do not ask if that is all he's got. This may be damaging to his ego. Generally, avoid shouting too much. It is not always a cute thing to do.

State something dirty

Don't request that your partner talks dirty when you are having sex. In the event that you need to begin dirty talking, at that point, simply state something dirty and he will get the idea and then respond.

Show confidence and say what you want

It's in every case best to be certain and clear in bed. Try not to be reluctant to request what you need and voice what you don't need. In the event that it's something you're appreciating, give it a healthy "yes", like they're satisfying a deep-rooted dream. In any case, if it's something you don't need – make that understood. Just keep away from apathy – nobody reads brains.

Try not to censure your mate's looks or execution. On the off chance that you need them to accomplish something in an unexpected way, talk in the positive and mention to them what you might want them to do.

Correspondence in the room isn't anything to avoid. Numerous individuals find that it upgrades their sexual experiences. Simply ensure that what you state can't be deciphered adversely. What's more, if it's not about the current movement, spare it for another room.

Do you smell something consuming?

For what reason am I accomplishing all the work?

However, whipped cream is stuffing!

I can't feel it!

I have an admission...

I'm exhausted.

It is safe to say that you are going to cum?

It is safe to say that you are in?

Maybe you're barely clumsy...

My ex cherished this!

Okay, stop! I gotta go.

That is no joke!

Try not to destroy my cosmetics

We should not kiss.

What number of individuals have you laid down with?

When might you want to meet my folks?

Would you be able to please pass me the controller?

You woke me up for that?

You're not hard enough.

Chapter 7

Keeping it hot

Visually connect as you talk dirty to your sweetheart

Young ladies love it when a man gazes their eyes while talking dirty to them. It shows that you are sure and that you discover her to be too alluring. All young ladies, including your sweetheart, love it when they feel want. What's more, since the eyes are the windows to one's spirit, gazing affectionately at them will show her that you truly want her explicitly, which will make her wet for you. Furthermore, in the event that you will do this with the correct sort of tone and strokes, at that point, you will get your young lady/sweetheart wet and pulsating surprisingly fast.

Once more, make sure to go slowly with your better half since it shows that you're not penniless. Hurrying things additionally shows that you are in it for the sex and that sort of impression will murder the sexual state of mind immediately. You can couple the dirty talk with a couple of kisses to a great extent particularly around her neck, lips, and navel. Once more, ensure that you are doing this as delayed as humanly conceivable.

Take as much time as necessary in light of the fact that your young lady/sweetheart isn't generally going anyplace. Really awful that the main way you can visually connect through content is by utilizing the eye emoticon –

which is pretty darn futile for this situation. In this way, all things considered, you would need to adhere to dirty talk since it brings about the ideal result. Once more, as the decree says, careful discipline brings about promising results. Along these lines, don't be apprehensive doing your examination and turning into a messaging master

Your sweetheart loves dirty talk in profound, masculine voice

The main way that your young lady or sweetheart will actually feel like a lady is the point at which you venture up and turn into a man! Despite the fact that they won't let it be known, young ladies or lady friends love it when their man talks with a profound, erotic voice particularly when they talk dirty.

On the off chance that you do this right, your better half will consistently get wet and troubled at seeing you. This will likewise happen at whatever point you send her flirty instant messages. That is the way solid a profound, masculine voice is. Your voice is equipped for giving your better half wild sexual dreams. Also, the way to getting that profound, Vin Diesel sort of voice is by unwinding and letting your masculinity dominate. Try not to surge when you talk dirty to her and thusly, all that will become alright as normally as it should be. Hell, you may wind up amazing yourself by pondering who the hell is talking to your better half when it's been you such time!

What's more, much the same as messaging dirty, talking dirty in a profound, arousing voice takes a great deal of training. You will, consequently, be needed to unwind and not get to contemplating it that much. You additionally should be alright with your better half and afterward the rest will stick to this same pattern.

Make sure the mood is right

You have to comprehend that your dirty talk should coordinate well with the mood. You would prefer not to consider your sweetheart a dirty name when she's had the most exceedingly awful day at the workplace. Get my float? You have to ensure that she is in the mind-set or, more than likely things won't work out as you had at first arranged. Take a stab at offering your young lady a back rub or offer to prepare supper.

At that point, feel free to set up a hot shower for her. While on that tip, you can get somewhat innovative and leave some red petals on the froth just as candles in the restroom. In straightforward terms, make her understand what's coming so when you begin to talk dirty to your young lady, you'll prepare her and trickling just for you in record time. Your young lady must have a melody or two that she considers as her top choice. It wouldn't hurt playing the melody your sweetheart loves out of sight while lying other than her, dirty talking her spirit away.

All things considered, you should set aside some effort to gain proficiency with the ability since it will wind up making your affection life multiple times in a way that is better than it is. Also, the equivalent applies while messaging your sweetheart. Dirty talk isn't tied in with shrinking away from the real issue yet going in for the murder.

Make yourself alluring

The dirty talk ought to be utilized to cause your better half to feel like she is going to have intercourse to a monster – in light of the fact that you are a monster! Talk about how you would adore for her fingers to run over your masculine abs while you are kissing her neck (or any place she loves to be contacted or kissed). What's more, as you talk dirty to your young lady, you can get it together of her hand and direct it to that one spot that you need her to contact.

In the event that you murmur in her ear about how you love her hands on your abs, direct those hands to your abs. Also, kindly, don't talk about abs particularly if your abs are, well, nonexistent. There is consistently that one spot that your sweetheart loves – utilize that. Join it into your dirty talk and lead her to it. Do this and your better half will cherish you for it. You can likewise do a similar dirty talk routine through content and let your better half consider you throughout the day.

What's more, when you return home, she will bubble as she hangs tight for you. One thing you have to completely comprehend about this one specific point is the need to back your cases up. On the off chance that you utilize dirty talk to make her wet and longing for you, at that point, you have to satisfy your dirty talk. In the event that you vowed to make her spurt – do it!

So, if it's not too much trouble let your dirty talk be an impression of what your sweetheart is anticipating getting. In the event that you will do this right, at that point, you will unquestionably be large and in charge and won't actually stress over her leaving you until the end of time.

Snuggle with your partner before the dirty talk

Nestling is an underestimated part of the dirty talk. What's more, obviously, that is the place where a great deal of men turn out badly.

At whatever point you and young lady are nestling, it gives the best an ideal opportunity to you two to dirty talk and strokes viably. On the off chance that you do this right, you will quite often get her wet easily. And keeping in mind that you talk dirty to your young lady, ensure you are holding her tight while murmuring in her ear. Don't hesitate to snack her ear cartilage while you are busy and your dirty talk will assuredly have exactly the intended effect.

Far better, your erection can "coincidentally" jab her back or butt, supplementing the dirty talk as your appeal gets total. Snuggling has been logically demonstrated to bring down feelings of anxiety. It would, hence, be an essential you'd need you and your young lady to be in as you talk dirty to her. Once more, be as delayed as could reasonably be expected and ensure that you're not compelling things except if you need to make everything abnormal.

Be flighty

In the event that you are the sort of fellow who can't reevaluate his dirty talk, at that point, chances are that your better half will discover you exhausting inside a brief time. Furthermore, when this occurs, your dirty talk game will turn out to be less successful and that sucks a ton. Interestingly, we as a whole have a lot of sources for exploring dirty talk for example the web.

On the off chance that you're bad at examination and reusing lines, you can generally be innovative and thought of your own. This is on the grounds that a relationship resembles a wellness venture. The second you quit taking a shot at your dirty talk, it turns out to be pointlessly unsurprising. Furthermore, the most exceedingly awful thing about resting on your dirty talk game is that there is consistently another man some place honing his dirty talk abilities prepared to utilize them on your sweetheart. Ouch!

What's more, in the event that you don't keep up, he may very well grab your lady from you with no exertion – in light of the fact that he is excessively smooth forever. Do a great deal of training for whether you pick text or talk dirty to her. The more you practice your dirty talk, the better you will be at talking dirty. It is additionally critical to take note of that there aren't any alternate ways with regards to such issues.

Send flirty messages

Aside from the productive dirty talk when in bed or in the kitchen or when you are out on a sentimental date, you likewise need to endorse your young lady to a portion of coquettish writings. Flirty texts are a little lighter contrasted with dirty talk. Obviously, playing with your young lady or sweetheart is significant. The specialty of enticement is better put as the craft of highs and lows. For example, in the event that you dirty talk your young lady today, take a stab at playing with her the following day.

At the point when you do this the correct number of times, at that point, you will definitely have her by her tenterhooks. This is on the grounds that she won't realize what's in store from you next. Unusualness is the means by which a man will possess an enormous bit of land in his young lady's brain. What's more, for the umpteenth time, being coquettish is something that sets aside some effort to dominate. In any case, fortunately it's something that is truly achievable.

Grab each other out in the public

With regards to dominating the specialty of dirty talk, you have to comprehend that there are things you have to use to make it viable. Aside from nestling with your lady, you can generally get things done to make her insane. Don't simply show the game when you text her yet ensure you are supporting it up with a ton of activity. Grab her butt in broad daylight, getting her unsuspecting.

And keeping in mind that she is as yet shuddering, you can talk dirty while snacking her ear. On the off chance that this doesn't make her drenching wet... truly, I don't have a clue what will. However, consistently recall that she must be your better half prior to pulling such a trick. On the off chance that not, at that point, you will just appear to be a weirdo – which is a no-no.

Make important enquiries

Before you begin talking dirty to your young lady, it is significant that you take some quality time turning her on. You can begin by posing her driving inquiries. These sorts of inquiries are those that will prompt her vibe like you are luring her without alluring her if you catch my drift. What's more, making her consider it is actually what will make her wet.

For example, you can message your better half asking her what shade of clothing she is wearing. Doing this will trigger her wild creative mind and in the blink of an eye, she will begin pondering you removing it from her utilizing your teeth. Ensure that the content is short and directly forthright. She will react by either disclosing to you the shading or making you surmise – the two of which are stunning talking focuses you can use to proceed with the tease.

On the off chance that you decide to message her, kindly don't try too hard. The more you text your young lady, the more you depilate her inclination to see you, which is a grave error that most folks do, shockingly. It is thusly significant for you to consistently message with some restraint. Along these lines, it will lead her creative mind going crazy, which is actually what you ought to consistently endeavor to accomplish. When you return home, she'll as of now be dribbling wet with her underwear pulled right to her knees, asking for you to slide in. That is the manner by which you realize your dirty talk game is on the ace level.

Give erotic massages

Something else you can do to your better half while you talk dirty to her is giving her a sensual back rub. Everybody cherishes a back rub. It can prove to be useful, particularly when you need your sweetheart to unwind and, you know, get slobbering wet for you. There are places you should be contacting while you talk dirty to your young lady.

Also, in the event that you do both the kneading and dirty talking the correct way, at that point, you will have literally nothing to stress over. Your better half will be wet and pounding surprisingly fast, which will make the employment a smidgen simpler for you. On the off chance that you don't have a clue how to give a back rub, at that point, it would be a smart thought for you to learn and will do as such as quickly as you can.

Conclusion

Figuring out how to talk dirty to your partner is just the start. There are endless variables that are basic in a solid and connective relationship; you nearly need to regard it as an all-day work. At the end of the day, you have to recognize the way that one person is not quite the same as another. It is, along these lines, a smart thought for you to figure out how to try things out.

Try not to be bashful getting over the edge with the dirty talk just to perceive how far your partner can take it. In the event that he/she can't take it, prematurely end the mission. However, on the off chance that your spouse can go further, you are in great hands then. If dirty talk feels like an insult to your partner, let it go and don't repeat it.

The equivalent ought to likewise apply with regards to contacting your young lady, particularly when you just started dating. You can either ask or, shockingly better, test during foreplay. All things considered, there are different things referenced on the rundown that your partner will consistently adore. Simply recollect not to constrain things since it generally has a method of reverse discharges.

At long last, these things require some investment, so never at any point be in a rush. Take as much time as necessary and make sure to gain from your mix-ups. That, my dear respectable men and women, is the means by which you make your better half happy and wishing for more.

Lightning Source UK Ltd.
Milton Keynes UK
UKHW010639020123
414708UK00014B/735